Harvest of Devotions

Moments of stillness in God's presence

Lisa Braddock

Wisteria Valley Publications

Harvest of Devotions
Moments of Stillness in God's Presence

Scripture quotations are taken from the
King James Version (KJV) of the Holy Bible.

Published by Wisteria Valley Publications
Printed in the United States of America

Cover design and layout by Wisteria Valley Studios
Creative direction by Lisa Braddock

ISBN: 979-8-9994338-4-8

For my Heavenly Father —
Thank You for the words You've spoken into my soul,
for the peace You've poured into my heart,
and for entrusting me to share Your love with others.
May each devotion bring glory to You
and light to those who read them.

And the LORD answered me, and said,
Write the vision, and make it plain upon tables,
that he may run that readeth it.
— Habakkuk 2:2 (KJV)

Introduction

This book wasn't planned. It was prompted.
Every word you'll read came from quiet moments when
God spoke to my heart and said, "Write it down."

Habakkuk 2:2 says, "And the LORD answered me, and said,
Write the vision, and make it plain upon tables,
that he may run that readeth it."
That verse has been the foundation of this work —
the reminder that when God speaks,
we're not meant to keep it to ourselves.

We are called to share His words, to speak His truth,
and to let His light shine through us. What you hold in your hands
isn't a collection of prayers or lessons — it's a record of moments
when God spoke, and I obeyed.

Some of these words came while driving down the road,
some in the stillness of early morning, and others in moments
when I least expected Him. But every one of them carries
His fingerprint.

My prayer is that every page reminds you that God still speaks—
and that His voice can turn the simplest moment
into something sacred.

— Lisa Braddock

Table of Contents

Table of Contents

Put God First—Always

This came to me suddenly, right here in the middle of my day. When the Bible says, "Put God first," so many people misunderstand what that really means. They think it means saying a little prayer when they open their eyes in the morning—checking the box—and then going on with life.

But that's not what He meant at all. God isn't asking for a moment; He's asking for our mind. He's asking to be the first thought before every decision, the whisper before every word, the peace before every worry.

He wants to be first and foremost—all day, every day. Not just a morning greeting, but a constant companion. Not an appointment, but a dwelling.

"And thou shalt love the Lord thy God with all thy heart, and with all thy soul, and with all thy mind, and with all thy strength."
— Mark 12:30 (KJV)

When the Cup Feels Empty

For about a week now, I've been asking God,
"Where are You?" Driving back and forth to work,
especially early in the mornings, is when He usually speaks to me —
when He shows me things, whispers to my spirit, fills my cup.

But lately my cup felt dry. Silent. Empty.
I found myself crying out, "Why have You left me, God?
Why don't I feel You anymore?"

And then today, no warning at all — as soon as I got in the car
and started rolling good, He started talking. Showing me things.
One after another. So many things I couldn't even keep count.

He reminded me of this truth: He has not left me.
He hasn't left us, friend. Just because we don't feel the tug
doesn't mean He's not there. Just because we don't hear
His whisper doesn't mean He's gone. That's where faith steps in.
We must believe His promise.

And then — right in the nick of time — He speaks.

3

He pours out. My cup is full and running over.
What I thought would be just one little drop turned into an
overflow of His presence.

"...for he hath said, I will never leave thee, nor forsake thee."
— Hebrews 13:5 (KJV)

It's Time to Get Up from the Cross

Some people stop at the cross.
They stand there, weeping at the place of pain,
never realizing that's not where the story ends.

The cross was never meant to be the destination —
it was the doorway.
That's where my Savior died for me, but it's not where He stays.
The cross was the place of sacrifice.
The empty tomb is the proof of victory.

I thank God for the cross — I'll never forget what happened there —
but I worship the One who walked away from it.
Alive. Risen. Reigning forever.

Too many still kneel at the cross,
holding on to guilt, shame, or sorrow,
when Jesus is standing just beyond it —
hands outstretched, saying, "Come walk in resurrection life."

If our Savior got up from that cross, if He walked away from
the tomb,

if He lives and breathes inside of us today,
then, friend, He expects us to rise too.

It's time to get up from the cross.
It's time to stop living defeated.
It's time to walk in victory.
Because the cross was never meant to hold you — it was meant to free you.

"He is not here: for he is risen, as he said. Come, see the place where the Lord lay."
— *Matthew 28:6 (KJV)*

Rhythm of Peace

I've been hearing it over and over in my heart lately:
Slow down, daughter.
Wait upon Me.
Trust Me to provide.

I keep trying to work myself to death—working long hours,
running myself ragged. But that's not what I'm called to do.
My calling is writing the Word of God, plain and simple.
And these books? They'll be blessed. I'm walking in what
He's given me. And He's been teaching me that faith is the key.

This morning, God gave me a living picture of what faith
looks like in action.

He sent a quiet reminder through a man driving a white SUV—
an older gentleman, steady and peaceful. The first thing I noticed
was the magnetic sticker on the back: Thank You, Jesus.
I've got one of those too... but mine's still sitting in a box.

This man—he didn't rush. But he wasn't slow either.
Everything he did had a rhythm to it. Peaceful. Intentional.

He loaded his groceries carefully. Dressed in jeans and a shirt.
Nothing Special. Car clean and well-kept—not brand new,
but blessed. He closed the tailgate gently. Then he did something
small—but meaningful. He pushed in all the grocery buggies
into the corral. Not just his, but the others too—the ones other
shoppers had left halfway sticking out, sideways, and scattered
around like it wasn't their concern. He straightened both rows,
took care of what wasn't even his. No fanfare. No audience.
Just a quiet servant spirit.

And I watched him drive off with that same peace he carried the
whole time.
God spoke all over me:
"This is what I've called you to do, my child. Trust Me.
Stop rushing. I've got you. Let Me lead."

"Rest in the Lord, and wait patiently for him: fret not thyself
because of him who prospereth in his way..."
— Psalm 37:7 (KJV)

Already Answered

Sometimes before I even whisper a word, I can feel Heaven stirring. I can sense that something has already shifted, already begun, already answered.

God doesn't wait until I speak to start moving—He's already ahead of me, setting things in motion that my eyes can't see. That's why when I pray, I don't have to beg; I just have to believe.

There are days when I've sat in silence, too tired or too broken to form the words. And yet, somehow, peace found me anyway. That's God, answering before I call. That's His mercy meeting me mid-breath.

Today my heart rests in this truth: my prayers don't echo into emptiness—they rise into the hands of a Father who already knows, already cares, already answered.

And it shall come to pass, that before they call, I will answer; and while they are yet speaking, I will hear."
— Isaiah 65:24 (KJV)

Harmony at Dawn

This morning I sat with the quiet. No clatter, no demands—
just stillness. The kind of hush that makes you notice the
tiniest things. I noticed the birds. Just as dawn broke, one sang...
then another... then another. Not a single harsh sound
among them—just perfect, layered harmony. I sat in awe.
Those little creatures weren't making noise. They were worshiping.

Even the birds know to begin the day with praise.

They don't worry about the branch they're standing on. They don't
store up for months. They wake up, lift their heads, and sing with
everything they've got—singing to the One who made them.

I believe with all my heart those morning songs are their hallelujahs.
It's not chaos. It's not coincidence. It's a choir. A heavenly one.
And I can't help but feel convicted... because how often do I roll
out of bed with complaints on my lips instead of thanksgiving?

If the birds can rise in harmony, why can't we?

Let us learn from the morning choir. Let us start our day not with fear or to-do lists, but with a whisper of worship. The birds don't sing because they've got it easy. They sing because they know Who holds tomorrow.

"Let every thing that hath breath praise the Lord. Praise ye the Lord." —Psalm 150:6 (KJV)

Strength

This morning, I caught myself trying to carry the whole world
again. Trying to fix things. Force things. Hustle and handle it all.
But God stopped me right in my tracks and whispered:

"You don't have to generate strength. I am your strength."

I took a breath. A long one.
Because I felt tired, and truthfully—I was tired.
But that's the moment it hit me:
God never asked me to be the power source.
He only asked me to believe.

We live in a world that tells us to "dig deep" and "push harder."
But God says something very different:

You don't have to drum up strength when you feel empty.
You don't have to pretend to be okay.
You don't have to have a plan before you take the next step.
You just have to do this:

Be still.

Obey the next thing He tells you.

And believe that He's already gone before you.

God is your strength when you're worn down.
He's your strength when you feel forgotten.
He's your strength when you cry in secret and whisper,
"I don't know how to do this anymore."

You don't have to know how.
You just have to know Who.

"Not by might, nor by power, but by my spirit, saith the Lord of hosts."
(Zechariah 4:6, KJV)

You Are Capable of More Than You Know

Life has a way of convincing us that we're small, powerless, or stuck. But God has placed gifts, strength, and resilience inside of you that even you haven't fully discovered yet.

Your limits aren't defined by fear, doubt, or even your past. They are defined by His power working in you.

Think of David standing before Goliath — a shepherd boy who didn't look capable of much. Yet with God's help, he accomplished more than anyone thought possible.

You may feel overwhelmed, but you are stronger than you realize. You may feel small, but you carry the Spirit of the living God. You are capable of more than you know — not because of your own strength, but because of His.

"I can do all things through Christ which strengtheneth me."
— Philippians 4:13

Step Out on Faith

We talk about faith all the time. It's a word we hear preached,
sung, and written about all through the Bible. It's a big word
to be made up of such few letters — but oh, how mighty it is.

Some folks even carry the name Faith, but how many of us
carry it in our hearts? How many times do we actually exercise it?

Faith isn't something you just talk about — it's something you
step out on. The Bible says that through faith, the sick were healed,
the blind received sight, the dead were raised, and devils were
cast out. And yet, sometimes we forget that same power still lives
inside us today.

There are people lying in hospital beds right now, unable to speak,
walk, or even open their eyes. There are others sitting at home,
afraid to even step outside their doors. But faith... faith is what
gets you up. It's what makes you take that next breath,
that next step, that next chance.

Faith is everywhere — waiting to be picked up, spoken, and lived.

The only way to obtain it is to step out on it.

So today, don't just talk about faith.
Step out on it.
Step out on the cloud of faith — and watch what God can do.

"For we walk by faith, not by sight."
— 2 Corinthians 5:7 (KJV)

The Leaf

It wasn't a perfect leaf. It had blemishes, scars, spots
where time and weather had left their mark. But when the
wind hit, when the road got rough, when the speed picked up—
it didn't budge. That leaf clung to the glass like its life
depended on it.

And right then, God whispered: "That's you."

You're not perfect either. You've got scars. You've got places
weathered by life's storms. But what matters isn't the blemishes—
it's that you're still holding on.

The enemy throws winds your way. Life rushes past at breakneck
speed. Storms, noise, and chaos beat against you. But here you are—
still clinging, still rooted, still refusing to be moved.

The Word says: *"That Christ may dwell in your hearts by faith...
that ye, being rooted and grounded in love"* *(Ephesians 3:17, KJV).*
And again: *"I shall not be moved"* *(Psalm 16:8, KJV).*

So listen, child of God: perfection isn't what's keeping you.
His hand is. His grace is. His love is. And that's why, through
every mile and every storm, you can say with confidence:
I'm still holding on.

It was right in front of my eyes...
God knows how to get your attention.

It could have landed anywhere. On the hood. On the roof.
On the side mirror. But it didn't. That little fall leaf—spotted,
blemished, imperfect—landed right in front of my eyes.
Dead center on my windshield.

Once, I would've turned on the wipers and knocked it off, annoyed
at the distraction. But not today. Today I saw it as a blessing.
A message. A mirror of my own soul.

Because just like that leaf, I'm not perfect. I've got spots.
I've got scars. I've been through storms. And yet—I'm still here.
Still holding on. Still clinging, even when the wind beats,
the road roars, and the storm rages.

That leaf preached to me:

You may feel small.

You may feel insignificant.

You may feel weak and weathered.

But child of God, you are still holding on.

The Word says: *"Fear thou not; for I am with thee: be not dismayed; for I am thy God: I will strengthen thee; yea, I will help thee; yea, I will uphold thee with the right hand of my righteousness." (Isaiah 41:10, KJV)*

That leaf isn't just a leaf—it's a testimony. A reminder. A blessing straight from Heaven: you don't have to be perfect to keep holding on. You just have to cling to the One who's holding you

It held on.

Eight miles down the road, that little leaf was still clinging. At the stop sign, it wavered, tilted like it might fall. But when I picked up speed, it flipped right back into place—dead center in front of my eyes.

It's not perfect. It's spotted. Weathered. Fragile. But it's still hanging on.

And the Spirit whispered again: That's you.

You may tilt. You may stumble. You may feel like the next stop will be the end of you. But when the journey picks back up, His hand steadies you. You flip right back into the place He purposed for you.

The Bible says: *"We are troubled on every side, yet not distressed; we are perplexed, but not in despair; persecuted, but not forsaken; cast down, but not destroyed."* *(2 Corinthians 4:8–9, KJV)*

That leaf preached a gospel:

The stop sign can't shake you.

The sun can't dry you out.

The wind can't rip you off course.

The passing world can't blow you away.

You are not perfect, but you are still held. You are still in place. You are still right where God wants you.

When a Leaf Speaks:

Some folks will laugh when you say a leaf spoke to you.
They'll roll their eyes, call you silly, or think you've lost your mind.
But let me tell you something, sugar—my God can speak
through anything.

He spoke through a burning bush *(Exodus 3)*.
He spoke through a donkey *(Numbers 22)*.
He wrote on a wall with His own hand *(Daniel 5)*.
And if He can do all that, He can use a little fall leaf to
preach hope straight into my soul.

That leaf said, "You're not perfect. You've got blemishes. You've been tossed by the wind. But you're still hanging on. Don't give up. Don't let go."

Here's the truth: *"The natural man receiveth not the things of the Spirit of God: for they are foolishness unto him... because they are spiritually discerned." (1 Corinthians 2:14, KJV).*

It takes an open heart and Spirit eyes to catch God's whispers in everyday life. Some will never hear it, but those who do will never forget it.

So when I get where I'm going, you can believe that little leaf's coming in this car with me. Not because it's just a leaf, but because it's a reminder that my God still speaks—through anything, to anyone willing to hear.

I Am David

Driving to work this morning, I didn't feel that usual word from the Lord that often comes to me on the road. But then, as I opened a devotion about King David, God began to speak.

David sinned greatly—he fell into adultery, fathered a child in that sin, and even arranged the death of an innocent man. Yet the Bible still calls him a man after God's own heart. Why? Because he always returned to the Lord. God forgave him, restored him, and blessed him—spiritually and financially—despite all his failures.

I realized today: I am David. I see myself in his story. Like David, I've sinned. Like David, I've fallen short. And like David, I've been forgiven, lifted up, and blessed by God.

The enemy tries to weigh me down with guilt, to make me feel unworthy, to keep me chained to the past. But the Word of God says: *"There is therefore now no condemnation to them which are in Christ Jesus, who walk not after the flesh, but after the Spirit."*
— *Romans 8:1 (KJV)*

So today I say it out loud: Get behind me, Satan. I am forgiven. I am blessed. I am a child of God. I am David.

No Vacancy for the Devil

You've heard people say, "You got the devil on one shoulder
and God on the other. "Well, honey, not me. I don't have room for
Satan to sit on my left shoulder — because God already owns that
property. He bought it and paid for it, and I'm not renting it out!

See, when you start renting space to the devil, he never stays
in his room. He starts taking over the whole house — your peace,
your mind, your joy, your family, your friends. That's what he does.
He's not a tenant, he's a thief.

That's why you've got to be firm. Let God own it all —
both shoulders, both ears, every part of you. He's the only one
who needs to be whispering in your ear.

And you can always tell when the wrong voice shows up. If it
brings fear, doubt, or confusion — that's not God. Rebuke it right
there and send it packing.

Don't rent your space to Satan. Post a "No Vacancy" sign on your
heart, your mind, and your home. You belong to God.

"Submit yourselves therefore to God. Resist the devil, and he will flee from you."
— James 4:7 (KJV)

Lord, thank You for owning every part of me — body, mind, and soul. When the enemy comes knocking, remind me who the landlord is. There's no room for him here.

Right on Time

Praise God! Praise God! Praise God!
I don't know why anyone wouldn't want to serve a King like Him.
He is always right on time — never late, never early, but always
in the very moment you need Him most.

Everything I've been praying for — peace, guidance, reassurance
that He's still carrying me through the storm — He answered
tonight in His quiet, perfect way.

When my heart grew heavy, He sent a message of encouragement.
When I felt unseen, He reminded me I was on His mind the
whole time. That's my God — faithful in the storm, gentle in the
waiting, and always right on time.

*"The Lord is good, a strong hold in the day of trouble; and he
knoweth them that trust in him."*
— Nahum 1:7 (KJV)

Hidden Hurt

Some people look polished, steady, and "all together." But just because the surface looks smooth doesn't mean the heart isn't breaking underneath. Quiet tears don't always fall where anyone can see them. Silent battles don't always get noticed.

The truth is—none of us are perfect. We're all walking around with cracks and scars, some healed, some still tender. That's why kindness matters. That's why compassion counts. Because you never know who is barely holding it together right under your nose.

So don't measure a person by the smile on their face or the neatness of their clothes. Measure them by the fact that they are still showing up. That they are still standing. That they are still trying.

"For the Lord seeth not as man seeth; for man looketh on the outward appearance, but the Lord looketh on the heart."
– 1 Samuel 16:7 (KJV)

And remember—while people may overlook your pain, God never does. He sees. He knows. He cares. And He will carry you through when you feel like no one else notices.

In God's Timing

Sometimes we want to rush in, to fix things in our own way, but it never works that way. Only God knows when a heart is ready. We can't know that—but He does. He sees the moment when someone is soft enough, open enough, willing enough to receive.

That's why it matters to stay in His presence, to walk close with Him. Because when you're in tune with the Lord, you will hear from Him. He will tap you on the shoulder. He will whisper with that small, quiet, peaceful voice: "It's time."

He's not going to shout it. He won't force it. But if you follow that gentle prompting of the Holy Spirit, you'll hear Him say, "It's time". God had already gone ahead of you. He had already tilled the soil of the heart. He knew the exact moment when the seed of love would be received instead of rejected.

You see, He has never left you. All through your storm, God is working. Never doubt that. Never give up. I have noticed in my life when break through is close, that's when Satan fights me hardest with giving up.

God is saying: "Let Me till the ground. I'm still working. Your job is to plant the seed. I'll do the tilling—you just be faithful to sow."

So don't quit. Don't give up. Joy comes in the morning. Joy always comes in the morning.

"For his anger endureth but a moment; in his favour is life: weeping may endure for a night, but joy cometh in the morning."
— Psalm 30:5 (KJV)

Who Are You Following?

Jesus said in *John 10:27 (KJV):*

"My sheep hear my voice, and I know them, and they follow me."

Let's read that again, honey — and they follow Me.

Not the pastor.
Not the choir leader.
Not the brother shouting the loudest or the sister who thinks she's most holy.

They follow Me.

Somewhere along the way, a lot of folks forgot who the Shepherd really is. They started chasing personalities instead of Presence. They listen to every new preacher online, every loud voice in the pews, every opinion that sounds spiritual — but they never stop long enough to hear the gentle voice of Jesus saying, "Child, I'm right here."

You can love your pastor. You can appreciate your church family. But they're not your Savior. They can point you toward the cross, but only Jesus can lead you through it.

And here's the beauty of His promise: He knows His sheep. Personally. Intimately. By name. He doesn't need a microphone or a title. He just whispers — and the ones who are His know that sound.

So today, ask yourself honestly: Whose voice am I following?

Because when you start following Him, the noise fades, the confusion clears, and peace steps in like sunlight after a storm.

"And the sheep follow him: for they know his voice."
— John 10:4 (KJV)

Lord, keep my ears tuned to You — not the crowd, not the stage, not the noise — but to the Shepherd who still calls me by name.

Let God Tend the Soil

We spend so much of our lives out there with a rake in one hand and a shovel in the other—trying to fix, to dig, to make things grow the way we think they should. But sometimes, that's not our job.

Sometimes, God whispers, "Lay it down."

Lay that shovel down. Lay them hard feelings down. And let God tend the soil.

You don't have to dig into it anymore. You don't have to keep beating the ground, hoping something will change. The truth is, all you're called to do is plant the seed.

And how do you plant a seed? With love. With mercy. With gentleness. You gently drop it in. Cover it lightly. Pat it. And walk away.

Then you trust that God's got this. Because He does.

He's the only One who knows how deep to dig, how much water to pour, and when the sun should shine. You just plant the seed—

He'll make it grow.

"So then neither is he that planteth any thing, neither he that watereth; but God that giveth the increase."
— 1 Corinthians 3:7 (KJV)

Not Hiding—Abiding

This morning, a sweet young Walmart employee asked me, "How come you're always hiding? "It caught me off guard—but I smiled, because I realized I wasn't hiding at all. I was sitting in my little corner by the tree, in the first spot on Row 1, letting peace find me. The world rushes and honks and hurries all around, but I've learned to drown out the noise and make room for stillness.

I'm not hiding. I'm abiding.
In that quiet space, I meet God. I hear His voice in the calm between deliveries, in the rustle of leaves, in the stillness He tucks into noisy places.

Father, thank You for showing me that peace doesn't have to wait for the perfect place. You meet me even in parking lots. Until my dream porch overlooks the fields, keep me content to sit beneath this little tree and hear Your still small voice.

"Abide in me, and I in you. As the branch cannot bear fruit of itself, except it abide in the vine; no more can ye, except ye abide in me."
— John 15:4 (KJV)

Just Pray

It's early in the morning, and as I drive, my mind fills with thoughts about prayer.

We make prayer too hard sometimes. We try to dress it up, make it sound holy, fancy, or proper. But God isn't looking for polished speeches—He's looking for you.

If you were sitting down with your child, your mother, or your best friend, you wouldn't worry about sounding perfect. You'd just talk. You'd open your heart. That's what prayer is — a conversation with your Father, your Friend, the One who already knows every word before you say it.

You can cry. You can laugh. You can sit in silence. He hears it all. He loves you with everything that is within Him.

Don't be afraid to talk to Him. Don't overthink it. Just pray. Ask, and you shall receive. Believe, and you'll see His hand move. Be thankful, be grateful, and always keep Him first.

Just talk to Him. That's all He's ever wanted.

"Pray without ceasing."
— *1 Thessalonians 5:17 (KJV)*

Thank You, Lord, for loving me enough to listen, even when all I can manage is a sigh. Teach me to come to You like a child, unafraid and honest, knowing You delight in hearing my voice.

An Inspiration of Hope

I spend most of my life on the road. Driving, sitting, waiting. And sometimes, out of nowhere, hope rises in the most unexpected places.

It may be the sight of a quiet farmhouse resting in the distance. Or fields of hay waving in the breeze, rows of corn standing tall, soybeans stretching across the countryside. Simple scenes — yet they stir something eternal inside me.

When I take it in, the weight of this world seems to lift. The heaviness dissipates. What replaces it is something beautiful: hope. It fills my heart, quiets my mind, and reminds me of heaven.

I don't know if hope is a cousin to peace, or if peace is the doorway to hope. But I do know that when God breathes it into your spirit, you feel it. You can't mistake it. It is Him whispering, "Hold on. I'm still here. I have good things ahead."

"Now the God of hope fill you with all joy and peace in believing, that ye may abound in hope, through the power of the Holy Ghost."
— Romans 15:13 (KJV)

43

No Room for a Pouting Spirit

You can tell when someone is carrying a bad spirit. It shows in their words, their posture, their eyes, and the atmosphere they bring with them. It changes a room. It drains peace. It doesn't take discernment to spot it—just a little time and a little truth.

Let's take pouters, for instance. Full-grown adults having pouting fits because they didn't get their way. That attitude is not of God—therefore, it is of the enemy. The "pouting spirit" is rooted in pride, self-pity, and manipulation. It's a quiet tantrum meant to control, to guilt, or to gain attention. And let me tell you, there's nothing godly, attractive, or anointed about it.

The Bible says, *"Only by pride cometh contention."*
(Proverbs 13:10 KJV). Pouting is nothing more than pride wearing a wounded face. It whispers, "I deserve better." It cries, "You hurt my feelings." But the truth is, it's a tool of the enemy to keep the heart turned inward, not upward.

A pouting spirit doesn't just make you look foolish; it reveals how immature you are in your walk with God. Spiritual maturity means you can handle disappointment with grace, not drama.

A pouting spirit cannot praise. It cannot worship. It cannot grow. It feeds on self, not on the Spirit. And that's dangerous territory. Because once we give room to pride, it opens the door to resentment, jealousy, and bitterness. Before you know it, that one sulk turns into a stronghold.

When we look at the Word, even Cain pouted when God didn't accept his offering: *"And the Lord said unto Cain, Why art thou wroth? and why is thy countenance fallen?"* — *Genesis 4:6 (KJV)* Cain let that spirit fester. He didn't repent or correct his heart; he let it harden. And what started as a pout turned into a deadly act of jealousy. That's how serious it is when we let our flesh lead instead of our faith.

You can't carry both the Spirit of God and a pouting spirit. They don't coexist. One brings peace, the other chaos. One brings humility, the other pride. One builds unity, the other divides.

So when that temptation comes to sulk, to stew, or to silently "teach someone a lesson," stop and recognize where it's coming from. The devil loves to disguise rebellion in emotion. He loves to make pride feel justified. But the Spirit of God calls us higher.

"Let all bitterness, and wrath, and anger, and clamour, and evil speaking, be put away from you, with all malice: And be ye kind one to another, tenderhearted, forgiving one another, even as God for Christ's sake hath forgiven you."
— Ephesians 4:31–32 (KJV)

When your heart feels heavy and your feelings get bruised, take it to the Lord, not to a pout. Because the moment you trade self-pity for praise, Heaven notices. The atmosphere changes. Peace returns.

Lord, if there's ever a trace of that pouting spirit in me, convict me quick. Don't let pride sit in my heart. Teach me to humble myself, to be thankful, and to walk in grace even when I don't get my way. I don't want to be ruled by emotion — I want to be filled with Your Spirit. Let my countenance reflect joy, not selfishness, and my attitude reflect Christ, not Cain.

Right in the Middle of My Mess

These words aren't written from a mountaintop. They're written from the middle — right in the tug-of-war between faith and frustration, between trusting God and asking Him why.

Some days, I feel strong. Other days, I feel like I'm barely hanging on. But it's in those moments I realize something: this is where the real harvest happens. Not when everything's blooming, but when the soil is being turned — when life feels heavy and the heart feels raw.

I don't write because I've arrived. I write because I'm walking it out, step by step, just like you. Sometimes I write through tears. Sometimes through hope. Always through faith.

If you've ever sat in your car and wondered if God still sees you... He does. If you've ever looked around and felt like your story's stuck in the middle... it's not. The middle is where He meets you. The middle is where the miracle starts growing.

"The Lord is nigh unto them that are of a broken heart; and saveth such as be of a contrite spirit."— Psalm 34:18 (KJV)

A Little Effort, A Lot of Heart

I'm sure you've heard the phrase a hundred times if not more —
"Kindness matters." Well, we're going to talk about it again.
Because it truly does.

It doesn't take much to make someone feel loved, cared for, or
respected. But it also doesn't take much to hurt someone's feelings,
either. Sometimes it's not the big things that wound people — it's
the silence, the ignoring, the lack of acknowledgment. And that
doesn't mean the person is too sensitive. It means you were
disrespectful.

Always, always check yourself. If someone sends you a message,
respond. Even if it's nothing but a little heart or thumbs-up emoji —
acknowledge them. If someone calls and you can't answer, send a
message as soon as you can to let them know you couldn't answer at
the time. It's so simple, but it says, "You matter."

If someone waves at you, wave back. Smile first. Don't wait. Take
the initiative. God tells us to be kind — not just to our friends or our
families, not just to our church crowd, but to everyone.

"And be ye kind one to another, tenderhearted, forgiving one another, even as God for Christ's sake hath forgiven you."
— Ephesians 4:32 (KJV)

Kindness isn't about grand gestures. It's about small, everyday choices that reveal what's in your heart. If you've got unread messages, unreturned calls, or people waiting on a simple word from you — take a moment and respond. Let them see the love of God in your actions, not just your prayers.

Because love that stays silent doesn't heal anybody, including yourself. Kindness isn't just a thought — it's a motion.

Just to See Jesus

I'll tell ya, it's somethin' how you can see the name Jesus, and it does somethin' to ya. You can walk through a store, pass a hundred shirts and signs, and not pay one bit of attention. But then—there it is. That name. Jesus. I don't care how small the print is or how far away it is, your heart just knows when you see it.

The other day at Walmart, the door greeter had a shiny new pin on. I took a double take and thought, that's Jesus! I believe it said "I [heart] Jesus," but truth be told, I couldn't tell you what the rest of it said. All I saw was Jesus. And right there in the middle of the store, my heart whispered, "Praise God. Thank You, Lord." It just makes me so happy to see His name show up everywhere I go.

We don't have to see Him with our eyes—He's still there. By faith, He's there. He walks with us every single day, morning, noon, and night. But you know, it's not just about saying His name. The Bible reminds us that not everyone who says, "Lord, Lord," will enter the kingdom of heaven. Anybody can wear His name—but it's what you're doing with it that matters.

Let's be the kind of people who don't just wear His name... we walk it, speak it, live it. Because there's power in that name—still healing, still saving, still changing hearts.

"Wherefore God also hath highly exalted him, and given him a name which is above every name."
— Philippians 2:9 (KJV)

When God Shows Up

I started to say, "I don't really have anybody." You see, I don't have a husband anymore but all my friends have husbands. My boys have their wives and families. And as proud as I am of them, sometimes I feel like a third wheel no matter where I go — even with my own children.

So there I was, letting my thoughts wander down that lonely road again, feeling like I just didn't have anybody. But before I could even finish that thought, God showed up.

All at once, He reminded me of every person He's placed in my life — my brothers, my sister-in-laws, my sons, my daughter-in-laws, my nieces and nephews, and my precious grandbabies — all eight of them! One by one, their names came flooding into my heart like warm sunlight breaking through the clouds.

That's just how God is. He doesn't let me sink into self-pity for long. He'll step right in and say, "Hold on now, child — look at all I've done for you."

And He's not done yet. Because the same God who reminded me of who's already here... is also preparing more people to cross my path. People who will love, encourage, and walk beside me.

So the time for feeling sorry for myself? Kicked straight out the door. God showed up — and that changed everything.

"The LORD will perfect that which concerneth me: thy mercy, O LORD, endureth for ever."
— Psalm 138:8 (KJV)

The Morning Ache

Every morning, before the sun even peeks through the curtains, I wake up with a lump in my throat — that deep ache that sits heavy in my chest. It's been there for a long time now. Some mornings I pray before my feet ever touch the floor, asking God to take it away. Other mornings I just sit still and breathe, waiting for that wave of sadness to pass.

It started the day my world shifted — when the people I loved most drifted away, when I no longer woke up to the sound of little feet running through the house. That's when the mornings got quiet... too quiet. And that's when the ache came.

I've learned something, though. That ache isn't punishment — it's proof. Proof that I loved deeply, that I gave my heart to people who mattered, that I poured out pieces of myself for my family. Sometimes love just doesn't have anywhere to go, and it settles in the heart as a heaviness. But God knows what to do with it.

So these days, when the ache comes, I whisper, "Here it is again, Lord. You know this pain better than I do. Please hold it for me." And somehow, the air feels a little lighter.

Because the truth is, the ache may visit me every morning — but so does God. And He's stronger than the ache.

"Weeping may endure for a night, but joy cometh in the morning."
— Psalm 30:5 (KJV)

The Seed of Compassion

Sometimes the only thing God asks us to do is plant a seed. Not a seed of judgment. Not a seed of criticism. But a seed of compassion.

It doesn't matter what someone looks like, what they've done, or what the world says about them. Pain is pain. Hurt is hurt. Tears are tears. And in that moment, what people need most is not our opinion, but our heart. God did not call us to judge. He called us to love.

When you stop, even for just a minute, to listen, to care, to comfort —you plant the seed of compassion. You may never know how deeply that seed grows in someone's life, but God knows.

So let's plant it. One hug. One kind word. One act of love. That seed can bloom into hope.

"And be ye kind one to another, tenderhearted, forgiving one another, even as God for Christ's sake hath forgiven you."
— Ephesians 4:32 (KJV)

God Will Provide

Well, here I sit. Off work again. Seems like I sure do miss a lot of work here lately. Well, praise God anyhow. There's always a purpose for what's going on.

The car's broke down again — back in the shop.
You know how it goes. You save money for tires, and then find out you need it for the engine instead. But even in moments like this, I've learned something: God will provide.

He always does.

Maybe not in the way we expect, or the time we hope for, but He never forgets His children. Sometimes He uses the breakdowns to slow us down — not to punish us, but to remind us that He's still the one steering the whole thing.

"But my God shall supply all your need according to his riches in glory by Christ Jesus."
— Philippians 4:19 (KJV)

Church Hurt Ain't from God

I don't know if some church folks even realize the damage they do. People walk through the doors looking for help, for hope, for a little love — and instead they get criticized for how they look, how they talk, or how they dress.

Honey, the Bible says plain and clear,

"Charity shall cover the multitude of sins." — 1 Peter 4:8 (KJV)

Love, not rules. Love, not ridicule.

There was a time when "church hurt" meant conviction — when the Word of God pricked your heart and made you want to change. But that's not the case anymore. Nowadays, church hurt often comes from people who think they're better than you. They expect you to walk their line instead of God's line.

And I'll say this straight: that spirit is not from Heaven. That's from Satan himself. The devil loves nothing more than a proud Christian who runs off a hungry soul.

You can't shame somebody into salvation. You can't insult them into holiness. You reach people by loving them right where they are — the same way Jesus did.

Some of these folks honestly believe you're bound for hell if you don't do things their way. There are even preachers out there saying a man will go to hell for having a beard. Excuse me? Oh yes, they do.

But last time I checked, they plucked the hairs from the cheeks of the Messiah — the same Messiah who had compassion.

And the last time I checked, we are to be like Jesus — the One who had the beard, who was full of compassion, forgiving, and loving.

So let's stop using God's house to break what He's trying to heal. Let's love people first — and let God do the changing.

Because real holiness doesn't wound. It welcomes.

"I gave my back to the smiters, and my cheeks to them that plucked off the hair: I hid not my face from shame and spitting."
— Isaiah 50:6 (KJV)

"He that saith he abideth in him ought himself also so to walk, even as he walked."
— 1 John 2:6 (KJV)

Look Up

I was driving down the road the other day with a heaviness pressing on my spirit. Just a little tinge of uneasiness that I couldn't shake. So I did what I always do when my heart feels weary—I looked up.

The sky stretched out in the prettiest blue I'd ever seen. And right there, in all that wide-open heaven, was just one thin, silvery cloud. Just one. And immediately, my spirit lifted.

The old saying goes, "Every cloud has a silver lining." That's not a Bible verse, but the Word does remind us where our hope is found:

"I will lift up mine eyes unto the hills, from whence cometh my help. My help cometh from the Lord, which made heaven and earth."
— Psalm 121:1-2, (KJV)

Friend, whatever cloud you're staring at today—big or small—don't forget to look up. The sky is still bigger than the cloud. God is still greater than the trouble. Your help comes from Him.

Look up. In Jesus' name, you'll feel so much better

Thank You

To my Heavenly Father —
Thank You for entrusting me with these words
and for never limiting where You speak.
You've met me while driving down quiet roads,
in the stillness of waiting when I'm parked,
on my walks beneath open skies,
and through the eyes of little children.
You've spoken in the city and in the countryside,
reminding me daily that Your presence is everywhere—
whispering truth in the ordinary moments of life.

To those who have prayed for me, encouraged me,
or spoken a word of hope when I needed it most —
thank you. Your faith and kindness have strengthened me
in ways I can't even explain.

To my family and friends —
your love and patience have been a shelter in every storm.
Your steady support has reminded me that God often speaks
through the people He places in our lives.

And to every reader holding this book —
Thank you for opening your heart to the words
God has given me to share.
May His voice speak peace and hope
to you in every season of your life.

With love and gratitude,

Lisa Braddock

About the Author

Lisa Braddock

Lisa Braddock writes from the quiet places
where God still speaks — in the hush of early mornings,
in the hum of everyday roads, and in the stillness of a waiting heart.
Her devotionals are not imagined; they are heard.
Each one began as a whisper from Heaven,
captured in ink so others might hear it too.

A country girl at heart, Lisa sees God's beauty
in the simplest things — the wind through the cornfields,
the laughter of a child, the clouds that drift like reminders of grace.
Through her writing, she hopes to help others notice Him again...
in the ordinary, in the waiting, and in the wonder.

Lisa makes her home in North Carolina,
where quiet moments and country roads often stir
the words God places on her heart.
She treasures time with her sons and grandchildren
and finds joy in life's simplest blessings.

Lisa is also the author of beloved children's books like
Willow Learns to Talk to God and
Diddle Daddle Jack: The Wild Wagon Ride,
as well as several forthcoming inspirational titles.

Her prayer is that through every devotional, readers feel seen,
loved, and gently drawn closer to the One who never stops
speaking.

www.ingramcontent.com/pod-product-compliance
Lightning Source LLC
Chambersburg PA
CBHW020803130626
46554CB00006B/2293